MW01226220

WHO MOTIVATES
THE MOTIVATOR?

ELIZABETH POLLOCK

Copyright © 2020/Elizabeth Pollock

All rights reserved.

ISBN:9798625856782

Published by Organic Art International LLC

Salt Lake City, Utah

A paperback edition of this book was published in March 2020 by Elizabeth Pollock. All rights reserved. Printed in the United States of America. No part of this book may be used or reproduced in any manner whatsoever without written permission except in the case of brief quotations embodied in critical articles and reviews.

DEDICATION

For Beatriz M. Keller de Antola, my mother-in-law, whose unwavering passion for reading and conviction has encouraged me to begin small and write.

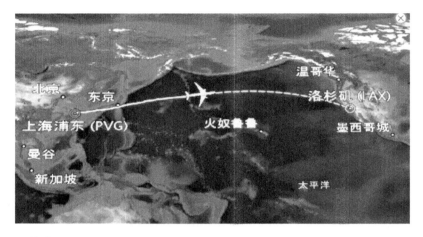

(iPhone screenshot returning from Shanghai in July 2019)

ACKNOWLEDGMENTS

I would like to express my gratitude to my mentor, **_Mary Lou Falcone_**, who has the priceless ability to listen and offer gentle suggestions of insight.

CONTENTS

I : Animal Instincts 1

II : Embarking on an Unknown Journey 2

III : Adrenaline Immersion...10

IV : Biomimicry - Uniqueness 11

V : Flexibility 13

VI : Stillness 15

VII : Rethinking the Way, We Think Things ® 16

VIII : Samsara - The Life Cycle 24

IX : Electricity 26

X : Organic Elements & Perspective..30

XI : Shifting 33

XII : Connection & Imagination..40

XIII : Balance 41

XIV : Money is a Motivator, or is it? 42

XV : Old Versus New...43

XVI : Recycle, Reuse, and Repurpose 45

XVII : Augmented Reality (AR) vs. Virtual Reality (VR): What is Real?
....46

XVIII : Chinese Culture 48

XIX : Traditional Customs 53

XX : "El Reproche" – Recrimination 57

XXI : Colors and Shapes 59

XXII : Shŏu=Hand 64

XXIII : Conclusion 67

About the Author..70

Note from Author: 71

I

ANIMAL INSTINCTS

"**L**ost in the jungle of green foliage, it's time for me to escape and discover the free-flowing water of a cool, refreshing treat to soothe the soul, especially my hooves," she said. "Shhh... come closer, I need to tell you a secret." She was waist-deep in the river with someone's handprint along one side of her. There was evidence of human interaction in this scenario, but no one was there. Who could it be? Where were they now? Why didn't the horse run away? Her black coat began to shine again as the sun reflected upon her body. She was content just being there at that moment. Her name was Dulcinea. Yes, that's right, the horse was named after a fictitious character in the novel written by Miguel de Cervantes, only, this Dulcinea was a horse that lived in Central America. The best way to survive the scorching hot rays of the southern hemisphere is... well, to go for a swim, of course! Splash!

(Rene Miro's handprints and horse, Dulcinea, in Chepo, Panama, Central America)

II

Embarking on an Unknown Journey

L et us begin at the current moment in my life: returning from China, having taught at Jilin University JULC in (Dongbei) in the northeastern region of China and then in Shanghai for an almost three-year journey. We chose to leave behind everything, from family to the comforts of home and old habits. This was a brave new beginning. No matter at what age we undertake such journeys, we are taking a leap of faith, so to speak. It would be easier to just stay put in our fishbowls. What we do know is that when we decide to swim in the ocean, a whole new world opens to us. So, don't look back. Just go forward—wherever the journey is supposed to take you. It is downright scary, especially if the country you choose to begin this journey on is one in which you do not speak the language. This journey is one of self-discovery and lots of changes. Change is usually something that most people want to avoid, but as we all know, change is inevitable. The more we push it aside, the more it comes back to us in different forms. Learning to embrace change is a skill or a muscle like any other in our human form that we need to exercise. So, if you decide to take that brave step and join the expatriate world, your whole being will transform as you embark on this path of self-discovery. This journey is both internal and external and is one of truth. Some call it faith. The more you face the unknown and unpredictable situations, the better equipped you will be to adjust to life no matter what the circumstances are. Traveling and learning about different cultures is fascinating and frightening at the same time. You continually learn about yourself, including what you can tolerate and what you can't. By making this move to another country, you can experience different cuisines and learn about the culture that will far surpass any expectations you previously had. You reach a new level of normal each day. This new world is a daily adventure conquering the unknown and navigating outside your own land starting with the language.

Let us think about our daily routine and what we cannot live without. Ok, time to wake up. Let's prepare for a cup of coffee. Oh no, the Chinese are not a coffee culture. It's all about the tea. Well, not to worry, I did know this before, so I came prepared with my ground coffee. However, for me, since space was a luxury and I was going to Northern China, the decision was a choice between a coffee grinder or a warm coat. Since the choice was obvious and logical, I began to train my brain to adapt to such traveling necessities and asked what I should wear first rather than what I should bring.

Our first stop was in Changchun, China, which at that time of the year was 26 degrees Fahrenheit (which is -3.33 Celsius) and snowing, so every inch of suitcase space was precious. Also, the Chinese are known for their petite sizes, so I did not know at the time if I would be able to buy anything in my size as far as clothing. Therefore, only the necessary items were placed in the suitcase.

(Harbin Ice Festival, Jilin Province - 50 minutes North of Changchun by train)

The Chinese language is a pictorial-based language and is quite complicated. Most individuals use the simplest form to begin speaking Mandarin Chinese, known as Pinyin. How would I communicate in China without speaking Chinese? Unlike romance languages, which you can pick up in a few months of intensive study, it takes years to be able to have a decent conversation in Chinese or to be able to sit in an academic classroom and actually understand what the professor is saying. Any language is much easier to grasp quickly when you start at a young age.

In this minification booklet, I'll talk about my three favorite passions in life: teaching, writing, and art. When I was not teaching, I immersed myself in either of the other passions. With the frequent practice of these hobbies, I began to transform myself, my behavior toward life and particularly teaching. For those of you who are professors, coaches, or parents, we all know that our cups need to be filled again in order to inspire others. Each picture tells a story about a time in my life when my inner being needed to be energized but was instead just drained. What do you do? Where do you go for inspiration and motivation? There are times when we all want to throw in the towel and quit, especially when teaching overseas. There is a myriad of challenges, such as language, culture, and different economic systems. Accessibility to teaching materials is crucial to education and keeping up with the reforms in a global world. How do you cope and take a negative situation and flip it around to have a positive outcome? My hope is that these illustrations, paintings, and words will ignite the fire in you to do whatever it is that you do better than anyone else and with your personal flair stamped upon it. We are all born with a special talent—a gift that we can share with others. Where do you find your motivation?

(Hangzhou, old temple hike to look out at the harbor, January 2019)

Teaching is a wonderful profession, which I found out later in life and have embraced for the last 10 years. A colleague gave me a gift that I cherish. It is a ceramic plate that reads as follows:

"Teachers who love teaching, teach children to love learning". [1]

Parenting is teaching, although we may not realize it at the time. *"Children learn what they live"*. [2] Each word, gesture, and action are being indelibly recorded in their moldable minds.

What is inspiration? Who inspires? Well, the answer is quite different for each person. It is personal. Like an art form, we as humans are metaphorically changed by our environment and situations. We have specific elements in life that motivates them to act or react. Teaching is a happy balance between the yin and the yang, pushing and pulling, like antonyms making perfect sense in a comparative story to show a reference point.

---

[1] www.naturallife.com, Robert John Meehan, 2016.

[2] Title of a book by Dorothy Law Nolte & Rachel Harris, 1972.

Art is inspirational; the dimension, the perspective, and how it affects our daily lives whether we are aware of it or not. It is inextricably woven into the composition of life just as light energy can be transported freely. It is a part of the elements of light and color that also affect the viewers' opinion. When looking at a piece of art, it is very subjective. People are dealing with their level and sense of reality, which can be very limited. The openness of a perspective on art or, rather, life is quite different. What is our purpose in life? What inspires us to move forward? That's the beauty of life; only we can answer that question.

A mentor, professor, and editor can encourage or direct us to perform our best. These are all motivational experts stretching us to the limits of human perfection. Enjoying time with family and friends can be both therapeutic and invigorating. Books can motivate us to start a project or reflect on the past in a positive way that may tap into an element of our past that we need to work on to help us move forward and not become stuck. To reinvent ourselves and grow is not an easy task, especially as we age, but it is essential to living a happy and healthy life. When we are not connected to this life and our awareness is foggy, which can happen from time to time, well, then we are just sleepwalking through life.

Having mentors is inspirational because they listen to what we say and give us another perspective on the idea or concept that perhaps we never thought of. A mentor can assist in reaffirming a belief in oneself—having us respond to the questions of who we are and what we are trying to accomplish. Providing this support is when a greater energy is called into action to suggest clearer explanations or more direct actions.

Albert Einstein's law of nature states that everything in nature has a vibration. We are made up of atoms and each atom has a frequency.

(Birdman sailing along the water canal in Zhouzhuang)

Becoming in tune with our own frequency or vibration can direct us towards fulfilling our purpose or mission in life. [3]

We take the reins and become focused on the task at hand, which is our growth as a person, *and* live up to our full potential—becoming alive from the inside out.

Seeking a mentor is a way to validate our path. Once we start in this direction, we almost always question why we waited so long or where we have been all our lives. I've been simmering. The willingness to let oneself simmer may be the most difficult aspect of developing discipline.

Growing up as a middle child and shy, I was always afraid of leaving the starting block too soon and being exposed to criticism. Having a mentor is like having a sounding board that can catapult us to the next level. Then, as the art project begins to take form, the inevitable doubt creeps in.

Once we experience doubt, we humble ourselves and realize we are only human beings. It's like having a balloon burst when we are so excited about a project, event, or outcome. It's that pestering voice, a naysayer, who speaks from a negative low point and holds us back from our

---

[3] www.https//Vasudev, 2015: Inner Engineering: by Sadhguru Jaggi

dreams. If only we could believe that we have supersonic powers, we could truly soar every day. Expect miracles!

In the following pages, you will see photographs, paintings, and a sculpture that was created during my years living abroad, mostly in Latin American countries, the Caribbean, and Asia. The last three years were spent in Northeastern and Southeastern China. When I was in the process of creating this art, I became focused on the task at hand, which

allowed me to express myself and live in the present moment. I was happy, despite some daily challenges that came with living abroad. Each image tells a story but it may express something different to you. Perhaps you were in a similar situation and handled it differently. It's all a matter of how we look at things. Is the glass half empty or half full? We cannot be perfect and cheerful every day of our lives, but as a teacher, it really helps to be a positive person and navigate with a healthy attitude.

Take one moment at a time, one step at a time, and stay focused on the job at hand. That is the only way this man will make it safely to his destination. He even invented and designed this bicycle to be able to carry this load. How creative? Easy does it!

(Ji'anian Road No. 8 Yangpu District outside Shanghai University of Finance & Economics)

(Westlake, Hangzhou tourist boats)

(Westlake model posing for the New Year, Hangzhou, China)

III

ADRENALINE IMMERSION

D ali, dali, dibujo, dibujo, dice el professor. Go, go on, draw, draw, said the professor. Here I was—with my Danish artist friend from the expat life 25 years ago—in an advanced sculpting class because they were not offering any beginning classes in drawing at the University of Panama. Oh, my goodness, what in the world was I thinking? I did not know how to draw, paint, or sculpt. And on top of that, I barely spoke Spanish. Talk about being crazy about my passions. As the old saying by Nike goes, "Just do it". Don't be afraid to try new things.

(Panama Sculpture of a woman model at the University of Panama, 1996)

IV

BIOMIMICRY - UNIQUENESS

O ur skin was tanned by the heat of the afternoon sun. We became tired from battling the wind, and the sun was beating down on our bodies all day. It was 5:30 pm and the sun was closing in on the horizon. The crabs were scurrying into nearby holes. We were starving but didn't want to leave this peaceful paradise, listening to the waves crash against the shore. The universal flow of life was indelibly inscribed in our minds.

The curves of the lines, the flow of the movement, and the shape that looks like a conch shell. It's a modern space-age minimalistic architectural wonder inspired by nature. Music, anyone?

(Symphony Hall, Harbin, China, July 2018)

Biomimicry - Symmetry

Splat flat across the pavement dead center in the middle of the sidewalk just stuck there, lifeless. The iridescent wings reflecting a rainbow of colors—mostly green—that could be seen by the naked eye. Frozen in time like a specimen shown under a microscope or under glass in a museum.

(Guoquan Neighborhood, on route to work at the University of Shanghai Finance and Economics)

V

FLEXIBILITY

The lush green foliage of the palm tree branches swayed effortlessly and without persuading either party to react and make a choice. Each turn we make in life can determine the essential elements of who we are and where we want to go. But remember, no decision is a decision and sometimes it is the best decision, like a palm tree swaying back and forth, not allowing anything or anyone to break it or twist its limbs. Painful bliss...

It took me a while to catch my breath. My heart was there on the beach. We were separated again. How long would it take to mend my broken heart? Bright cumulus clouds embellished the skies as the turquoise waters glistened in the foreground. A soft afternoon breeze cooled our bodies, rejuvenating the air and negative space. Ahh! 40 days and 40 nights of organic natural vitamin D at its best. Now that's motivational...

(Acrylic painting on wood; carved out this scene before I knew we were going to live there. The British Colonial Hotel on the beachfront in Nassau, Bahamas)

VI

STILLNESS

W e could hear the screeching of the cicada bugs in the still and humid Guyanese air. The sound of those insects was so annoying that I tried to muffle it by listening to some music. Instead, the vibrations of these irritating bugs reminded me of the sound of aluminum foil being crinkled up in a ball. Through the stillness of the night, nature gave me an idea for tomorrow's recyclable art project. Voila!

(Family art project made in British Guyana by Luciano & Miguel, 2004)

VII

Rethinking the Way, We Think Things *

U pon notification of my acceptance to teach in China, I knew it was going to be a challenge, especially because I did not speak Mandarin. This challenge would be totally different from my experience in Latin America since I do speak Spanish and know the culture well. When you do not speak the language of any culture, you are automatically at a disadvantage. Understanding and speaking a language of any culture surely helps in understanding the culture—from how they think to what motivates them. So, I knew that my teaching approach had to be unorthodox. How would I be able to teach most of my students who were Chinese? An acquaintance who later became a good friend recommended I learn Pinyin. [4]

Pinyin is the foundation of learning the phonetic system for transliterating Chinese. It is the basic sounds taught to children or beginners who want to learn the language before mastering the character part of Chinese. Pinyin uses the letters in the Latin alphabet. There are 409 sounds in Chinese, and 4 basic pitched tones and a fifth neutral (toneless) tone.

Hanzi, on the other hand, is the written system of the Chinese language and is at least 3,000 years old. Usually, this writing is more difficult for most people and is the last element to perfect.

---

[4] http://www.blog.tutorming.com/mandarin-chinese-learning-tips/what-is-pinyin. Hua, S.L., October 19, 2015.

The HSK exams are the tests that are a gauge to understanding your proficiency level in Chinese. There are six levels of this exam and it is divided into two parts—the oral section which is a test for your pronunciation and proper tones, and the written section that deals with the character writing.

As I struggled for weeks, then months, trying to grasp something and be able to memorize the language, I discovered that in order to be able to relate to these students, I would have to use a visual method first. Since Chinese is a pictorial language, and I discovered the only way to effectively communicate with my students and be able to gauge whether or not they were grasping the language was through visualization. Then, once the mental picture was in place, to reinforce this approach with a pedagogy.

This pedagogy refers to the theory and practice by teachers who instruct in English as a Second Language (ESL), and English for an Academic Purpose (EAP), whereby a scaffolding approach is used to formulate an appropriate level lesson plan. First, start off the class by listening to a dialogue of a conversation. Listen again, giving the students a fill-in-the-blank worksheet. Next, teach one new grammar focus and incorporate the lesson to revolve around that session.

The teacher divides the lesson into four parts: a reading, writing, speaking, and listening section and the material is seamlessly incorporated into the lesson plan. Pronunciation practice is incorporated through a game, drill, and/or skit. This is the final 30 minutes of the class and will aid the teacher in diagnosing who is the benchmark student.

A linguistic method I learned was at the Lado Institute in Washington D.C. The total approach method has been taught for over 50 years and is still used today. Its usefulness has been proven to be successful since the diversity in the classrooms now is more international. Some of my students were from various countries in Latin America, specifically Columbia, Venezuela,

Brazil, and Chile. Others were from Egypt, Yemen, Malawi, Russia, China, and Japan.

Creativity and the arts allowed me to express concepts visually when words at first were not understood. Little by little, this visualization and gesturing communication became the key element in my pedagogical approach to teaching.

(Think on your feet! Siberian Tiger, Harbin, Jilin Province, China)

How do you rethink a class when the students are all looking at you with open mouths or sleepy eyes, or are plain uninterested in the subject?

When we speak, what we say and how we say it are important as a professor begins to teach a new subject matter. What is especially important is how we introduce the material or how we go about a review of the textbook when studying for an exam. When we begin to teach a concept, it is helpful to ask thought-provoking questions. By knowing how much the students already know about the subject matter, we can adjust our level of entry or advancement about the topic.

It's a constant struggle to keep ourselves positive all the time. Teachers, lecturers, and professors are like actors on stage, waiting to be called on cue. It is essential to have a positive attitude to motivate others. Through this attitude, we are also inspiring ourselves to be the best people we are capable of being. How can we do this every day? Well, by having a bag of tricks. Having an inventory of tools that you can rely on is essential and a key element to a successful classroom.

With today's global classroom and access to massive amounts of information via our cell phones, many educational systems are coming to realize that reform and the process of education is just as important, if not more important, than the information itself. This is especially true when it comes to the system of memorization. As Plutarch, a Greek philosopher, said, **"The mind is not a vessel to be filled... but a fire to be kindled."**[5]

For example, when we as teachers need to complete certain requirements of material to be taught, as well as deadlines in which to meet, we must be flexible and eliminate some concepts to meet those academic administrative demands. This requires analytical skills by the teacher right from the start of the semester. Also, taking into consideration the ability of each student's level of English, we adjust the curriculum.

Not to cast aspersions on any ethnic group, but note in a positive observation, in general, Asians have an incredible ability to memorize just about anything. This ability is very good for some things, but when it comes to speaking English in a colloquial way, it may make it difficult for a student to present an impromptu speech. We as human beings do not memorize everything we are going to say in any given situation throughout the day. Such memorization is a bit robotic and may lead to unnatural flow in a conversation.

---

[5] www.https//Greeka.com, Plutarch.

(Nanhu Park, Changchun, North East China, Jilin Province)

Academic environments should always be open to discovery, meaning a certain amount of time should be given for the students to interact with each other after new material is introduced. Particularly in English as a Foreign Language (EFL), English as a Secondary Language (ESL), or English for an Academic Purpose (EAP) environments, new material needs to be practiced and perfected in order to utilize and understand what it means in English. This process is called the facilitation stage in teaching or lecture. This presence of being is essential in any speech, given a specific environment or communication exchange. We need to know our audience when giving a speech. For example, when you know you are speaking to 200+ audience and the majority are not native English speakers, then you would choose the vocabulary wisely and articulate very well.

The lecturer should have a good lesson plan, a clear direction in which to guide the students, and also, we hope, engage them with respect to the material to get a reaction and to know what is it that they are learning and what is it that they need to have explained further. This is called the facilitation process, where we can see and judge how many students are truly grasping the material.

We need to be able to think on our feet. Life is sometimes like an impromptu play, so mastering this spontaneous reaction to everyday circumstances is extremely helpful. To be able to apply what we learn and paraphrase the lesson into colloquial English is essential in the learning process.

In Eastern cultures, specifically China, most students are excellent at prepared speeches and essays that they know the question to beforehand. When it comes to anything impromptu, most of them find it exceedingly difficult to think on the spot because of China's educational system of repetition and memorization. Bendability is the key to mastering any non-prepared play or speech.

(City of Zhouzhuang, part of the water town outside of Hangzhou)

Many people use the five senses to perceive life, whereas others use their sixth sense. Blind people or individuals who are left without a sense usually become much more sensitive to their surroundings and their perception is elevated. Do we really practice a daily awareness of our environment through our senses? Breathe, smell the roses, look at your daily surroundings.

Close your eyes, ring a soft bell, start listening to the dynamic rhythm of these Gregorian Chants from the Monks of Notre Dame. Repetitious sounds invoke calmness, peace, and clarity in learning. Don't be in a rush to make conclusions about anything. We perceive things through our five senses: this is the way we experience life. When we are teaching, we do not know all the answers. Professors cannot know

21

everything, so leave a 5-minute segment at the beginning or end of each class to make a statement about something to which you don't know the answer.

This facilitation process, particularly when teaching English as a second language class, is important to the learning process. This is the time for daily feedback. You can open it up to the students as a debate topic, which becomes a way to provoke interactive communication skills and to learn more about your students. What do they think? What is their critical thought process? Saying you do not know opens the infinite possibilities to know and learn more about yourself and the topic.

Music inspires and energizes. The composer, Ludwig van Beethoven's, Symphony number 5 in C minor begins with four notes. Imagine these four notes are repeated. Sometimes, short-short-short-long notes are softer then louder. Why is this music so famous? Some may remember it was the victory song during World War II. Most people remember this piece of music because of its raw power and simplicity of these four notes. This famous composition was known for the overwhelming way it represents a triumph over adversity[6]. Just as famous classical compositions can motivate us, so can music in nature inspire us.

My alarm clock each day were birds singing at 5:30 am outside my window. It is true, I did not set an alarm clock. These organic sounds woke me up smiling and happy each day, even on the weekends when I knew I could rest longer. Imagine, in a bustling city such as Shanghai of 25 plus million people, the respect for nature and use of electric cars is unprecedented. We can all learn from this model of how to change our cities to become self-sustained eco-systems.

Respect for age and nature. Look here, who knows how old this tree was before it died? If nature could talk, what stories would it reveal?

---

[6] Kerman, J. & Tomlinson, G. (2008) p.231-233

(Moganshan Road Art District, Shanghai - M50 an old tree stump)

VIII

Samsara - The Life Cycle

Hands up, gather around. Now, let's hold hands and move away from each other, forming a large circle. Wheels go around and do not stop until someone stops them. A life cycle stops for a moment when someone dies and those close to their loved ones must somehow move on, as difficult as it is; otherwise, they will be living in the past. Life continues without regard to our human feelings even after someone dies. This life cycle is called Samara.

(Tube construction wheel at the University of Finance and Economics, Shanghai)

The symbolism of the wheel has many meanings, from eternal life to the representation of the sky and the earth and the continuous energy of the universe.

When a child is born, he or she begins to recognize shapes. The round shape symbolizes the parents or caretakers. Children adore any kind of ball to toss and spend endless hours in constant movement, throwing it back and forth and never seeming to tire of this repeated exercise. This familiar circular form gives comfort and stability for the child to confidently continue to discover and trust the world.

IX

ELECTRICITY

T he quietness of the night triggered peaceful sensations in the air. I was bathing the children upstairs in the bathroom. After a hot tiring day filled with countless activities, their eyes were suddenly sleepy. The power went out! This was a normal occurrence, but this time, I was upstairs with the children and one slipped away, headed for the stairs. My heart started to pound. My body began to boil. I didn't know what to do… I took a deep breath! Quickly, I invented a game where they had to come close to hear about the knight in shining armor.

(Lotus flowers in bloom, British Guyana, 2000)

(Cheddie Jagon Research Center, Georgetown, Guyana (wooden structure with Demerara shutters, named after one of the rivers). Home of Primer of British Guyana in 1961-1964)

Electricity can be a motivator and an inspiration. "Let there be light".[7] When light shines upon something or someone, the subject becomes alive.

New York is not the only city that doesn't sleep at night. As we know, everyone is unique in their human traits. One trait that we perhaps rarely think about is whether a person functions better in the morning or at night.

As we age, some of us tend to retire early, missing all the excitement of a night life. For teenagers, exploring the night life is a whole different perspective on adulthood. Nighttime is sometimes associated with fear, darkness, the unknown, and mystery—perhaps even evil.

---

[7] Genesis: 1:3

(The Shanghai Edition - Marriott Hotel, 199 Nanjing Road, Huangpu, Shanghai)

Art can inspire us in many ways, whether it be looking at modern art in a museum or listening to an orchestra. The beauty of art is that it is interpreted in unique ways by each person who experiences it.

'Clouds' from Three Nocturnes by the modern composer, Debussy, depicts an element of surprise. A hallmark in music was set by this composer for his whole tone scales. Having subtle, blended, and mysterious shades of tone in his music. These dreamy art qualities were also used by impressionist painters of the same era. Specifically, Claude Monet's paintings may invoke vague, unclear images that inspire us while others see a dreamy view of a serene countryside that relaxes us.

When listening to Debussy's music, some listeners are uncomfortable by the night surprise in his music. While others welcome these sudden sounds of mystery. By elevating our sense to experience art, we are allowing ourselves to express our reaction to it.

Shanghai is an electric city that definitely has a pulse. The city is safe and very convenient to travel in alone, even if your Chinese is limited. So, get out of your element of comfort and explore your environment at night. For teachers in China, this activity will surely add a whole new dimension to your experience there and subconsciously affect your lecturing sessions. A fresh perspective is what global educators and reform needs, especially with the massive changes we are going through with technology in every facet of our lives.

How can we incorporate the cell phone into the classroom? Teaching the new millennials or Generation Z, as they like to be called, is quite a challenge but also pushes us as educators to a whole new level. Many games and new apps can be incorporated into the classroom to assist the professor, especially in large classrooms. These applications can help us see how present and participating the students are and to what extent they are understanding the lecture.

In smaller classes, games may be used to lighten the mood when massive amounts of information are being presented. Teachers may test the material in half the class. Also, using these phone games is a good way to include all the silent or unfocused students. Bonus points and early leave time are beneficial to encourage a healthy competition but mostly participation and engagement is what I am looking for.

Keep them open-minded and alert. Insert a short video that can lead to a conversation or debate. For example, this one: close your eyes, listen to what you hear. If you could describe what you just listened to in one word... what would it be? Use a Venn Diagram or write these words on the board.

X

Organic Elements & Perspective

"To be or not to be,[8] that is the question". "To be" is one of the most irregular verbs in the English language. To be living in the present moment is easier said than done. Living in our awareness and taking an inventory of our surroundings and ourselves should not be underestimated. Children always live in the magic of life, those blissful joyous directionless spaces in time that can never be repeated. Let there be light...

It's late in the day and the clouds have sunk lower, allowing the sun to penetrate between the open cracks in the old cement coal mill. Old versus new grows a pleasant surprise—how the rusted rock shafts look, creating a sense of autumn color. Light in its organic form is truly a motivator, creating clarity, design, and a pure sense of natural art uncompromised. The Art of being!

---

[8] Shakespeare, William, Hamlet, 1599.

(Outside West Bund Museum, old mining structure on the Yangpu River, Shanghai)

We all know that, depending on our attitude in life, we see the glass as half empty or half full. Here, a child may start counting the squares that are reflected by the negative space of the sun and may not see the old industrial tracks of the coal mine.

When we are feeling stuck in whatever place or moment in time, just remember there are always several solutions at any crossroads. We can use grammar to get us unstuck... that's what antonyms are for... what's the opposite? If it is a picture or sculpture, turn it upside down. Now what do you see? Just as an antonym can change our perspective of a picture, so too can a story being read backwards from end to beginning. The elements have shifted; the focus is reversed.

(Walking along the Yangpu River outside the West Bund Museum)

XI

SHIFTING

" **A**s you are shifting, you will begin to realize that you are not the same person you used to be. The things you used to tolerate have become intolerable. When you once remained quiet, you are now speaking your truth. Where you once battled and argued, you are now choosing to remain silent. You are beginning to understand the value of your voice and there are some situations that no longer deserve your time, energy, and focus."

Love—what is love? True, unconditional love of anything or anyone: nonjudgmental and totally present in a moment in time. The happy moments in a fairy tale when you go to sleep with a smile on your face, knowing that love is the true healer of any situation.

Who remembers Woodstock? The music concert in the 1970s was the largest nonviolent gathering of all types of people in the history of the United States. Why was it successfully executed? The answer is love and compassion and the pure cooperation of humankind, regardless of race, age, nationality, or sexual preference. It's amazing what peace, love, and rock 'n roll can do.

An example of this happiness can be seen in a joyful child. Joy, excitement, and exuberance are a state of well-being. Usually, when we are feeling love, nothing can change our happiness, even if we are physically sick.

A child is licking an ice cream cone in the summer, only to find out there is more ice cream melting on their hands and clothing because they are swirling around looking at the kites flying in the sky. Youthful innocence is a beautiful thing to witness. Laughter is a positive gesture that we need to have more of in our daily lives. This joy of teaching needs to be demonstrated in a natural way to the students in order to get their full attention. Laughter inspires us to continue even when we want to quit.

A teacher is always on call, ready, set... showtime, acting like a monkey playing on cue. It is the most rewarding job, but at the same time, it is draining—physically, emotionally, and spiritually. Teachers always need sources of inspiration because others are learning from them. One of the reasons I love teaching is because I learn academic knowledge about subjects. More important to me, though, is that I learn about myself.

Teaching/coaching keeps me in balance. Some days, I am really good at getting my point across and have prepared my lesson plan like a pro; and other days, I doubt my abilities and say, am I a good teacher? We begin to learn about ourselves by first accepting our flaws and then embracing our strengths. The rewards that we receive are priceless and make this whole education field feel so fulfilling. How do we keep going and become an inspiration every single day of our teaching lives once we enter the classroom? We must orchestrate a motivational lecture and inspire so many students all at the same time. Let's go—it's showtime!

(French Concession, Taikang Rd., Dapuqiao, Huangpu, Shanghai)

The French Concession is a municipality located today in the Huangpu and Xuhui Districts. It is a large area bustling with activity from specialty clothing shops, boutiques to a wide variety of restaurants, museums, and exhibitions. At night, this area comes alive with outside musical activities on the streets as well as in some restaurants. This area of Shanghai started to emerge as the French Concession in 1849 until 1943. After WWII, it expanded in the late 19th and 20th Century, making it a modern cosmopolitan city.

(French Concession every afternoon plants get refreshed)

Historically, Shanghai is a fascinating city. During WWII, it housed many Jewish refugees who had nowhere to go and no official documents. A Jewish doctor by the name of "Big Nose" was a hero in his time during this period as he assisted so many civilians. At the Jewish Refugee Museum, the Chinese make a tribute to him. His name is Jacob Rosenfeld who moved to Shanghai in 1939. Shanghai was known as a haven for Holocaust victims during Hitler's reign. When you watch the film of many of the Jewish families who had all their possessions and official travel documents stolen, it will bring tears to your eyes. Thank goodness the Chinese demonstrated a human act of kindness and were open to allowing the entrance of these refugees and not deny them a place to live because of no official documents.

Living in China, I developed an immense admiration for this ancient culture and gathered inspiration from my environment.

(Longhau Temple, Shanghai, July 2019)

(Tea house in my neighborhood – located on Zhenli Rd. and my apartment was around the corner on Guoquan Road)

(Oldest Temple in Shanghai, first built in 242 AD)

(Turtles sunbathing outside Longhua Temple)

Modern China is known globally to embrace the Western ways in city designs and is demonstrated by their modern bullet trains to contemporary architecture in buildings. It is so different from the West with regards to plagiarism, particularly the United States where we have laws that protect individual ideas, inventions, and works of art.

Before the Tiananmen Square events in 1989, the leadership of the Communist Party was heading into establishing the foundation of a democratic society.

However, after the massacre at Tiananmen Square, the country fell in the other direction. Instead of a fully open democratic society, it resulted only in an open market for business under the *tutelage of the party*. China has brought consumerism to the next level.

Major cities in China have changed immensely over the last 30 years since implementing an open economy. Shanghai has gotten a facelift, from a flat city to now a bustling city with super modern skyscrapers resembling Western and other cosmopolitan cities. It is now a fusion of Western and Eastern culture—in both architecture and cuisine. The art scene is electric and pulsating every minute, with galleries and exhibitions in parks and museums all around the city, day, and night.

Shanghai is a modern, cosmopolitan city, combining the old with the new China. When you look from the Huangpu River downtown where the space needle is, you are not sure where you are. My first impression was that it looked like Hong Kong because of the water access, but then I saw architectural-style buildings like in London, Paris, and New York. It is a walkable city, with eateries everywhere to suit all budgets. One District of Shanghai is called the French Concession, where the streets are lined with large trees called Fagus, Beech, or French Phoenix Trees. The French brought these trees with them when they settled in the city in the 19th century.

In Buenos Aires, similar gigantic trees line the avenues and mark the borders of the parks, streets, and major thoroughfares. They are planted not only because of their large physical presence as prominent landmarks, but also because the roots demand so much water that they can absorb large amounts of water from torrential storms and prevent flooding in the cities.

XII

CONNECTION & IMAGINATION

W e as human beings are all connected somehow through our history and through our DNA. If we trace back our ancestry far enough, we can discover various cultures that we did not even know were a part of us.

In the well-known book, "The Little Prince" by Antoine de Saint-Exupéry, the young boy asks the adults to identify a picture. He asks them, "Does this picture scare you?" "Why no, of course not," replied the grownups. "It looks like an old hat," said the adults. "Really?" In fact, it was a drawing of a boa constrictor who was digesting an elephant. You can rest assured that a child's vision is totally creative and imaginative. Imagination is everything! It's one thing no one can ever take away from us as human individuals.

(Amsterdam – seven bridges – Amsterdam is the quintessential city of canals and is considered the Venice of the North. It also has the largest number of bridges in the world)

XIII

BALANCE

A little more to the left. Now the right. Wait, put this package in front. It's lighter and fragile. Ready, set, go! It's that time of the year again. Yuck... crunch time, final exams, research papers, etc. Sigh... How can we accomplish all this?... one step at a time.

Easy does it. It is all about the balance. Whether it be physical, mental, or psychological balance; it all comes into place at various times in our lives.

What is weighing you down? Just as a heavy load can weigh us down, so too can it motivate us to work through all our tasks to come to a finish. By reaching this point, we feel inspired by what we have accomplished. One step at a time. Just put one foot in front of the other. Begin at the beginning, just start.

(Daily business outside Fudan University, Shanghai)

41

XIV

Money is a Motivator, or is it?

Money is the root of all evil, or is it? Everyone is motivated by something; after all, we are human, right? Some people are motivated by other people, places, or things. Have you ever heard of the expression cash is king? Cash is a universal language.

Whatever country you are in and there is a language barrier, you can be sure that money will speak for itself. Be careful to know the cultural etiquette before flaunting your money, especially in a restaurant. In China, for example, leaving a tip of any amount is highly insulting.

(The official name for Chinese currency is Renminbi. It is abbreviated RMB, also called yuan, aka CNY. In Mandarin money is Qia′n)

XV

OLD VERSUS NEW

G eometric shapes rise above the ground in shining gold. Just because the gold architecture is smaller does not mean it is of less importance.

What materials did the people use to build the old structure back then? How long did it take them to complete the project?

It is helpful to do many things simultaneously to keep a healthy balance of positive energy, guiding us to create art. A generous balance among love, physical activity, and intellectual learning is a necessity and the key to living a fulfilling life. To be alive every day and enjoying each moment is difficult, especially when life throws us a curveball. But by having this healthy, supportive lifestyle, we can catapult into whatever it is that is in our universal experience at any given time. We know in order to live life fully we need to work through the negative times to be able to handle a blissful moment.

(Jing'an Temple,1686 Nanjing W. Road, Shanghai, China)

Walking in the park across the street, there are lovely gardens and a famous Thailand Restaurant which has amazing food. Jing'an Temple in modern-day China and a modern-day office building. The original date the temple was built is c.247 AD. However, in the Southern Song Dynasty (1127-1279), it was moved to its present location. It houses in Mahavira Hall, the largest pure jade portrait of Sakamuni. It stands approximately, 12 feet high. Imagine this temple stood long before all the audacious skyscrapers.

XVI

RECYCLE, REUSE, AND REPURPOSE

(Guoquan Road, across the street from my apartment)

The price we must pay for doing the right thing!

XVII

AUGMENTED REALITY (AR) VS. VIRTUAL REALITY (VR): WHAT IS REAL?

S ome technology is an invader of the mind. It has become an addiction for some new millennials, but it can also be used as an inspiration in the classroom. Teachers need to relate to their students. Currently, we live in a world of augmented reality.

Who has not dreamt of living in a utopian society? Social media sites are changing our channels of human interaction. The platform experts keep users glued to their cell phones like a dopamine pleasure as they unconsciously press "likes" as a response to continue the addiction to technology 24/7.

Currently, a new trend in China is for Chinese students to use their Pinyin name, choose whatever city and country they want to be associated with their WeChat app, and post another person's face for their profile picture. Then, when they show up in class, they are unrecognizable because the girls and guys dye and/or curl their hair and use color contacts like they were in some avatar virtual reality movie. The inspiration for this behavior has evolved through reading and watching the Anime fictitious characters created by Japanese artists as well as other global movie trends. The influence of these computer characters has changed some of the students' dress trends. Technology has caused some students to become so addicted to virtual reality games that when the millennials are in the classroom, they have a difficult time distinguishing what is real from what is virtual reality. Are you my students or cyborg students? Yes, we are living in augmented reality with all the apps, WhatsApp, WeChat, Google maps, etc., but VR is certainly not reality.

(Anime characters, Japanese artist)

XVIII

CHINESE CULTURE

In many respects, modern cities in China are years ahead of Western culture, particularly the United States regarding transportation technology. The transportation sector is newer and is the state of the art. For example, their trains are among the most rapid in the world. The Chinese came to Boston about 50 years ago and asked Siemens Company about their trains. The Chinese copied them and perfected them. These bullet trains are enjoyable to ride and connect people from the outer territories in less than one hour or slightly more from any direction. It is truly an incredibly comfortable and economical way to travel to different cities within China.

The Amtrak train that runs along the east coast of the United States is about 50 plus years old and is in dire need of updating. The safety is also questionable. There have been many accidents because of inadequate maintenance.

(Shanghai University of Economics and Finance September 2018)

University of Shanghai Economics and Finance campus set for electric cars, January 2019.

For the last four years, all you need to carry in China is your phone, anywhere from Beijing to Hangzhou to Shanghai to Harbin. Even in a smaller city like Changchun, which is in northeastern China, about two hours from the Russian border and has a population of about 3.5 million, it is not necessary to carry a wallet. Through the application of WeChat and Alipay, you can swipe your phone and pay for a rental bicycle on the street or a Didi (which is equivalent to an Uber), or a meal in a restaurant. No cash is needed. You can buy virtually anything from e-commerce to vegetables in markets to transferring money to your family in other parts of China. Everything is linked through your bank account. The convenience is amazing. Students cannot live without their cell phones. They even order take-out food during their breaks and find it ready when class is dismissed for lunch—hanging on tree limbs outside the classroom.

The whole economic model in China is that of a visionary. The model was first discussed at least 10 years ago. How can a country with so many people to manage, feed, and educate be so far ahead of Western culture in a short period of time? It has only been in the 30 years or so that the semi-free economic system has exploded in China. It is incredible the advancement of a modern city in such a short amount of time! We have not even discussed the issue of noise pollution. The cities should be louder with vehicle traffic noise, but there is hardly any. There is no buzzing of cars or bikes because almost everyone uses electric cars, bikes, and scooters. On my usual way home from the University on a rainy day, I was always fascinated to see the agility and coordination of motorbike drivers. One hand on the wheel, the other holding an umbrella, then a child on the back holding their daily groceries. It is some balancing act.

(Alipay bikes and Mo bikes, Guoquan Rd., Shanghai. Swipe with your
WeChat, which is a Chinese app on your iPhone)

My route on the way to the University each day, come rain or shine.
There was a bus line directly from my doorstep that dropped me off in
front of the University. It was about a 20-minute walk, bike, or take a
taxi or Didi. Most days, I walked or rode a bike.

(Hardware shop on Guoquan Road, Yangpu District, Shanghai)

Who needs a window when you can already see right away what
kind of hardware you need? Talk about efficiency and organization.

Zhangjiakou Section of the Great Wall of China. They happened to be filming a movie there in August 2016. I was lucky to have my picture taken with a beautiful 19-year-old model.

What makes The Great Wall of China one of the New 7 Wonders of the World? A Norwegian named Stephen Robert Loken, a 42-year-old hiker, took 601 days to walk the wall but only the section built during the Ming Dynasty (1368-1644). The oldest section of the wall, called the Zhangjiakou section, was built during the Zhao Dynasty (1045- 221 BC). This section is the steepest; it took me 3 hours to climb only one small portion of the section and 30 minutes to walk down, leaving days of wobbly legs, especially my calves.

There are many sections with differing levels of steepness to this wall, ranging anywhere from outside of Beijing to the sea on the coast near South Korea stretching 2,000 miles long.

Every day at the same time, lunchtime begins, and everyone is present, enjoying a home-cooked meal together.

We all know just one little word can change the whole meaning of a sentence. Let's take the word 'unbelievable'. What is so amazing about this word is that it can have a positive or negative connotation. Also, there are words that sound the same but have quite different meanings. These homonyms are used often in theater performances to depict a funny scenario and make us think.

Many of us are on the hamster wheel, working nonstop, especially in the United States where a one or two-week vacation is the norm. Most times we are too busy to just BE in the present moment. The children's book, "What Does It Mean to Be Present?"[9], talks about the difference between homonyms of physically being present and a birthday present.

Being in the present moment sounds so silly and simple to do, but believe it or not, many of us are thinking of what we need to do next or going over what we did earlier that day that we could have done better. We forget to just be. To be present in the moment is a joy.

---

[9] Orio & Wheeler, "What Does it Mean to Be Present?", 2010.

XIX

TRADITIONAL CUSTOMS

These giant fish, hanging there lifeless below the metal bar like a piece of artwork. The birds began to chirp despite the neighbors still sleeping. The air had a coolness that depicted the changing of the season. Christmas was upon us, but this year, we were celebrating in China on a different day.

(January 2019 outside my apartment in Guoquan Road, Yangpu District, Happy Chinese New Year!)

Outside, using whatever space was available, we were drying fish—a Chinese tradition.

Happy New Year! When we think of the New Year in the United States, we think about rich, delicious food, spirits, a Christmas tree, parties with friends and family, all waiting for the ball to drop-in Times Square.

Well, in China, they have parties, too, but they begin with the food process. For weeks, these fish hung outside to dry. The fish are packaged as a snack or meal to be eaten during the festivities.

Obstacles

According to Sir Isaac Newton's 3rd Law of Motion, "Every action has an equal and opposite reaction."

Obstacles are opportunities. When we are teaching a difficult class with difficult students or with too many students or with a challenging subject matter, we can always use a myriad of suggestions to change it up in the classroom each day. It's just a matter of perspective and always trying to be alert and aware in the classroom. Like athletes who stay focused on their bodies, so too must we as teachers become focused on our mind, body, and spirit. Some athletes call this the privilege of pressure. By overcoming these obstacles successfully, our reward as professionals will be that we grow and learn so much about ourselves. We have pushed the boundaries beyond what we thought we could do. We have stretched our students as well as ourselves to transform into the best people we can become in life. That is what the reward is for us as life coaches.

Captivation—How to keep your students in the 21st century captivated each day on a difficult or complicated subject matter?

Well, if you read Mandarin, this menu will be appetizing otherwise. If you do not read Mandarin, well then all you have to do is take a photo with your phone and hit scan and the application will automatically translate the menu for you rather than be surprised after you order anything.

An engaged classroom of students should not resemble some Gregorian Chant with homophonic texture but rather a symphony orchestra playing Ludwig van Beethoven's Symphony #5 in C Minor. How can those iconic four notes have so much memory and energy? This is one of the most recognizable pieces of composition.

Everyone has a different interpretation or story of their own to contribute to the classroom. Keep your mind open to all possibilities in education: the inspiration could come from anywhere.

There are so many applications now for students to answer questions and/or play games on their iPhones. Segment a time or special day by allowing students to use their phones occasionally in class. This will keep them alert and let the instructor know who is participating and who is not. After all, for these University students, the iPhone is a permanent appendage.

Creativity—How much is too much?

In today's classroom, to be effective in your approach to teaching, you will need to have a balanced curriculum mixed with creativity. An effective classroom is where students are engaged, interested, and asking questions. By using creative approaches to learn, you can draw innovative conclusions where everyone is participating, and it is a good way for you as a teacher to see how the individual is applying the knowledge. A creative approach also allows for varying your teaching methods and alternating innovative ways to keep the information fresh and new.

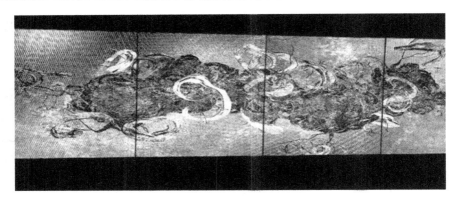

(Team Lab Exhibition at Tank Shanghai West Bund Museum on the Huangpu River)

Who can tell us what this painting means to you?

Keep students in constant motion, or at least in their minds.

(Child in front of Jiao Tong University enjoying being in movement)

XX

"EL REPROCHE" – RECRIMINATION

K nock, knock... "Come in," said the lawyer, "please sit down." Have you ever been in a situation where there was a heated debate with recriminations flying back and forth? Yes, then you can relate to this amazing piece of art.

Fear motivates. Don't get to the end of your life wishing you had done something you always wanted to do or without at least trying to do it. Take that vacation, sing that song, really listen to the music inside your head and fear nothing. Even scared cats have nine lives. The worst thing you can do is to not try at all. Even if you do something horribly, at least you have tried. It takes courage to take the step to perform what it is you have always wanted to do. There is tremendous growth in taking that first step. The seed is planted and grows, which is what we are meant to do on this earth. I would always tell our children that the most difficult thing in life is to grow up and change. Be brave and put yourself out there. If we do not grow, we just exist. We were not born to just exist. Even one-cell organisms change. Plants and trees change and become something so big and beautiful with long limbs and beautiful blossoms. Seasons are made for change. After the harvest is when we gain the benefits of our hard work.

("El Reproche", Oswaldo Vigas, painting sold at Sotheby's 2012 Auction)

XXI

COLORS AND SHAPES

S hapes like the Samsara wheel of life can inspire. Colors can also initiate thoughts or actions. Green signifies many things: nature, life, freshness.

(Wheatgrass in its organic form served at a restaurant in Shanghai)

In the Western world, we usually see this as green grass shoots that are put into smoothies.

Colors set the mood or atmosphere. According to Colin Ware, who wrote "Information Visualization", He discusses in depth about color and how this affects our perception. Colin Ware says color helps us break camouflage. Just like green can automatically send a signal to the brain to mean nature, life, and freshness. Blue can also immediately give us the impression of an ocean or a sky.

For example, saying the word, "world" to Chinese students without a visual means nothing. The "w" is difficult to pronounce. So, by showing a visual object simultaneously like a globe, and using synonyms for the object will automatically put the correct image into the students' minds so there is no misunderstanding and you can move along in the lesson. If you were good at the game, charades, then that will help immensely with teaching any foreign language.

Visualization is a language to the Chinese. Each stroke represents a word or group of words, so what better way to teach this Eastern culture about the English language than through visualization and storytelling?

In today's educational systems, we still tend to overload on content, which is useless unless the students can apply this new information. The last thing a teacher wants to do is to give his or her pupils more information, especially if some are incapable of digesting what the terminology means and are unable to explain and use this new information in a practical real-life situation. Each pupil needs to make sense of the information, to tell the difference from what is important and what is not. This sense-making can be encouraged through the facilitation process. Students can be divided into groups to practice using information in the correct way. Once the basic concepts (e.g., the rules of the English language) are understood, it is then the teacher can build on this blueprint.

Specifically, when teaching English as a second language (ESL). Dr. Robert Lado of the Lado Institute in Washington, D.C was an American expert on modern linguistics. He served as the Dean of the Institute of Languages in Washington, D.C. Doctor Lado has a specific methodology that has been proven successful. He retired as a director of Georgetown University over 40 years ago.

In today's classroom, students' mastery of the content of the material taught needs to be checked to evaluate whether the English or business concepts are being used properly. English is difficult enough with all of the rules and exceptions, not to mention the pronunciation.

When introducing a grammar focus into a lesson plan, it should be one grammar concept. Introducing multiple grammar points only makes the student more confused.

For example, according to Dr. Lado's "Total approach" to speaking English as a second language, this is where the four elements of listening, speaking, reading, and writing are all incorporated into a classroom teaching.

This methodology is used during a two-hour lesson broken down into two sections. After the dialogue is listened to, the next material taught is grammar. Usually, prepositions, phrasal verbs, and exceptions to grammar rules are the most difficult to grasp. So, in each lesson, we will be mastering one of these concepts.

Depending on the results of the class and the benchmark student, you can choose to move to the next grammar focus.

Practicing and implementing dialogue can be assessed using a facilitation process usually timed toward the end of the class or the second 45-minute interval in university classes. It is almost like riding a bike. Telling learners what to do is not the same as having them do it themselves. Give basic instructions, model these instructions, and then have the students use their knowledge of the information to actively practice the techniques that have been presented. Practice makes perfect sense. It is easier for students to work with their peers in a real-life situation using information that has been memorized and/or set out in a written script and practiced to be able to respond in a natural way, as in American colloquial English.

Some refer to this technique as "flipping the classroom", where the students express their interpretation of what was taught. It can also be useful in more advanced English-speaking classes. Giving the students an article about a world issue for homework and then having a classroom debate the next day.

What are we really preparing our students for in the work world? Yes, it is essential to be able to apply academic knowledge such as technology, business, or any other social science subject properly in the classroom or real-world environment. However, nowadays, young students go from undergraduate to graduate work and some on to obtain their doctorate degrees. This is very commendable, but students accumulate staggering debt in the process and lack practical knowledge of the real world. Today, students need hard skills and soft skills to be effective in the workplace. Particularly in the area of soft skills, today's Generation Z youth tend to overuse their phones and are unable to communicate effectively. Being a good communicator is the number one trait of a good employee—meaning being able to send coherent texts, emails, writing, and drawing if necessary, and excelling in face-to-face communication skills. In other words, listening and getting along with others. In the workplace, there will always be at least one person who is not exactly the easiest to get along with, but it is very important to know how to play a part in an office situation and carry on for the greater good of the project and the company—putting personal opinions aside.

There is a myriad of skills required to obtain a University degree that, of course, will vary depending on the field of expertise. However, a common core course in any field of study is communication. In say, engineering, these skills can include advanced mathematics or good computer programming. Most important of these hard skills in any field of study and work is reading and writing. If English is not a student's first language and this student is writing a paper, native English speakers should read it to ensure the author has effectively communicated what he or she intends to say.

The world is changing so much with all the new technology and there are no signs the pace will slow. So, with this change, our new generation of professionals must be adaptable and must understand who and what are participating in business and education. Reform is here to stay. Change is a good thing, although sometimes it is difficult to adjust to until we see promising results. Globally, we have great diversity in cultures and languages. Speaking two or three languages will become the new normal, just like it has been for generations of Europeans. Being culturally aware and speaking two or three languages will become more important than having an advanced university degree without any other experience.

XXII

Shǒu=Hand

T ouch is one of the five senses we use to interpret life. Gestures express a word, a thought, and or an action. What is so fabulous about them is they are silent and can speak for themselves. Remember back in the day when you entered the library as a child and the librarian would place her hand in front of her mouth with her index finger pressed to her lips? Yes, we knew exactly what to do.

(Shanghai's outdoor sculpture garden, May 2019)

Who motivates the motivator? We are all inspired by different things. When we become burned out when teaching, we must, like an artist, try a different approach, another angle that will provide a deeper understanding.

Change is inevitable and to live happily, our perspective needs to be open and flexible so we can ride the wave of evolution. It could be the evolution of the product you represent, or it could be the evolution of you as a person and how you have grown from your experiences as a teacher or business executive.

I am motivated by my students to become better at reaching those who look lost. On the flip side, the students who are very participatory and engaged in class are also a huge inspiration for me to step up my game and give them more challenging concepts or projects.

Pain, loss, and struggle can also be motivational. In times of adversity, we may not realize that is exactly what we need to be catapulted into the next new growth opportunity. It is easy to get stuck, to feel sedentary in our teaching, career, and family life. Why should we change? It's okay where we are now and, besides, we think we know our jobs well and experience no daily challenges. However, if we really want to explore and stretch ourselves to become the best at what it is we do best, it is necessary to reach for the stars. Put yourself out there to take a challenge into the unknown territory. The results of our efforts can surprise us.

Taking a break, sabbatical, or vacation is something altogether different. We can recharge our batteries by taking a time-out. That is different from just existing day to day, month after month, year after year, doing the same thing. Spice your life up a bit! It does not take much. Try a new recipe. The worst that can happen is that you will make a not-so-flavorful dish.

Teaching is a reciprocal career enabling both the students as well as the instructor to create, grow, and learn all at the same time. Teaching is an extremely rewarding career in many aspects. It is necessary in today's global world with the advancements in technology that we as educators continue to use unique techniques that will encourage students to become confident articulate speakers; good communicators, and well-rounded international citizens.

(Sohue Resort, Jilin Provence, 2 ½ hours from the city of Changchun, China. July 2018)

Teachers use pedagogy and a methodology that are effective but do not necessarily require us to be robotic about how we teach.

How do we inspire ourselves and others? All good leaders know that to transform others, you must first be willing to be transformed. The secret is within you! We all oversee our own destiny. Practice self-love and respect in the small tasks of the day and you will be blessed with abundance.

In the end, we must motivate ourselves to inspire others and that can only be done by experiencing each day, each moment with full awareness of our surroundings and interactions with people. Knowing ourselves and what inspires us is the best way to fuel our souls with innovative ways to create a newness to our present situation, whatever that may be.

XXIII

CONCLUSION

So, what is the common thread that makes us motivated? I would like to share with you my favorite quote on self-belief and self-love. Each time I read it, it brings tears to my eyes, especially when I've accepted a posting overseas and will be transported OUT of my comfort level. It is this fear that drives us to be the person we are supposed to become. The best version of ourselves.

Deepest Fear poem by **Marianne Williamson** associated with Nelson Mandela because he read it during one of his powerful speeches:

"Our deepest fear is not that we are inadequate. Our deepest fear is that we are powerful beyond a measure. It is our light, not our darkness that most frightens us. We ask ourselves. Who am I to be brilliant, gorgeous, talented, fabulous? Who are you not to be? You are a child of God. You're playing small does not serve the world. There is nothing enlightened about shrinking so that other people won't feel insecure around you. We were born to make manifest the glory of God within us. It's not just in some of us; it's in everyone. And as we let our own light shine, we unconsciously give other people permission to do the same. We are liberated from our own fear our presence, automatically liberates others."

It is a privilege and a blessing to be able to live outside of your own country.

(Sohue Ski Resort container, Jilin Province in Northern China)

In the above image, you will see a 40-foot container. Most expatriates use these containers to transport their belongings around the globe.

Where is home? The excitement of moving causes stress. When will our possessions arrive? Where will we live? When will we sell our car? What will we take, leave, or give away? These are the essential questions you repeat in your head. All these questions you will ask yourself before, during, and after you are settled in that country because you soon realize that you will not permanently settle in the foreign country unless you want to call it your home. The process begins again if you decide to return to your native country.

The importance of prioritizing and eliminating frivolous things when packing is vital in the moving process. The things we say we cannot live without are usually things we soon realize we **can** live without. They are just physical possessions we want to travel with us to make our lives more comfortable. What are we afraid of forgetting anyway?

Nowadays, ecologically friendly people are using empty containers to reduce the carbon footprint. Why not? They are lightweight, recyclable, and easy to use as a foundation structure for a home.

Home is where you are! When you choose to be an expatriate and live outside your own country, you have chosen to explore the unknown.

You have surrendered to the predictable routines of daily life. You have chosen to grow outside of your comfort zone. The forces of nature that live in the universe will guide you as to your next step. To go with the flow is living in the moment and stretching yourself beyond the unimaginable. They say if you can imagine or wrap your head around your dream... then it is not big enough.

To be fearless is putting one foot in front of the other and just expect miracles to happen. Always strive to do your best in whatever task it is, even menial tasks have great significance.

ABOUT THE AUTHOR

Margaret Elizabeth Pollock was born in Ridley Park, Pennsylvania in the United States of America. This is her first minification. The paintings, photographs, and sculpture are a partial collection of nostalgic memorabilia during her last 25 years of travel in Latin America and Asia. Elizabeth would like to thank her husband and sons for allowing her the sabbatical to pursue this writing.

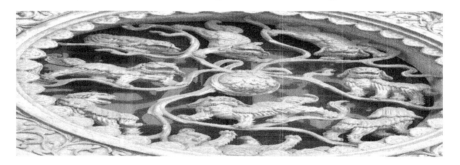

NOTE FROM AUTHOR:

Dear Reader, I hope you enjoyed this book; please feel free to add a review on Amazon.com. ***Who Motivates the Motivator***; Click this link https//amzn.to/39QyA7O, scroll down to my biography, and leave a customer review. Thank you very much for your support.

Organic Art International will continue to provide contemporary emerging trends that can aid in your life transformation.

Other books now include:

Rethinking the Way, We Think®, The Power of Introspection, Reinventing Yourself in Times of a Shifting Paradigm.

www.amazon.com/s?k=luis+antola+%26+elizabeth+pollock+rethinkin g+the+way&ref=nb_sb_noss

Both available on Amazon.com

Made in the USA
Middletown, DE
18 October 2022

12992216R00046